Arbor

Encore

Arbor

Encore

Collected Poems
Volume 5

Richard Gartee

LAKE & EMERALD PUBLICATIONS

Copyright © 2023 Richard W. Gartee
All rights reserved.

No part of this publication may be reproduced, in any form or by any means, without the prior permission in writing of the publisher, except for brief passages in a published review.

Published by Lake and Emerald Publications, LLC
Gainesville, FL
www.lepublications.com

Library of Congress Control Number: 2023922753

Paperback ISBN: 978-1-7363957-5-2

Front cover photo by Dieon Roger

Poems in this volume were first published in *Ann Arbor Review,* Copyright 1970, 1974, 1975, 1976, 1977, 1979, 2013, 2014, 2015, 2016, 2017, 2018, 2020, 2021, 2022.

for Allen Ginsberg
(1926–1997)

Contents

Foreword x
Preface xii
Arboretum Daze 1
January Moon 2
Time Koan 3
Spring Into Summer 4
On a Shady Lane 5
Purty Yellow Daisies 6
Fifteen 9
Soda Fountain Days 10
Flying in Eights 12
The Lion Has Flown 13
Last Lovers In Burgundy Province 14
Found Naked Lunch 16
River 17
Mountain Breathing 18
The Deva 20
Bananas for Baba 22
Tea in Goa 25
Shakespeare's Garden 29
First Revelation 30
Stay Seated 31
Four Lines for Ken 32
Stillpoint 33

Old Order	34
Brave Voice	35
Fame	36
Semi-Native	37
Lost and Found Shoes	38
Fingering The Jam	40
Summer Breeze	41
Laurel Canyon Houri	42
Last Dance of the Year	44
To Wish Again Upon A Star	45
He and She	46
Blinds and Shutters	47
Madwife	50
Enuf	52
The Mind	53
Grasses and Houses	54
Ever New Morning	56
Clouds	57
Unity	58
Cornfield Christmas	59
Sense and Probability	60
Un-Platonic Solids	61
Nothing Out of Something	62
Inspiration	64
The Poet	65
About the Author	67

Foreword

by Fred Wolven
Founder and Editor,
Ann Arbor Review International Journal of Poetry

Opening Richard's poems…

Long ago, whether a poet makes a conscious effort or not, I concluded that nearly every poet quite naturally creates at least a partial autobiography in his/her poetry or at least contributes in their poems what may later become part of such. As one reads through this collection of Richard's poems you'll find him offering significant bits of information and thus insight into his life by sharing his view of his and our world with the rest of us along with an introduction to the roots of his poems. And such glimpses of the world prove fascinating as he treats young love, writing poems, traveling (*Lovers in Burgundy Province*, enjoying winter snow in an *Arboretum* in *Ann Arbor*, taking in *Miami Beach*, or a *Poet* working anyplace).

A true working writer whether fashioning classroom textbooks for teacher-student use, or creating novels for pastime reading, or a poetry volume, Richard is one of a few full-time authors, along with a children's book writer and a musician composing lyrics for performance I have the pleasure of knowing.

In this volume Richard has an easy yet fascinating means of handling language as in "*black stalks, barren, tall: /gentled, lent charisma, / by the contrast with/ brown-russet bricks*," and "*A fawn noses aside a clump of snow / to nibble the spring grasses / flattened by the unexpected / slide of the powdery blanket.*" Or there's the ease with which his images fill line after poetic line: *"The poet's dark chocolate eyes / stare out her apartment window, / through a hard tropical rain..."* and *"The river starts wide, / then enters a chasm that narrows it. / Channeled between rocky walls, / its intensity increases, / cutting deep..."*

Also sprinkled throughout Richard's poems is more of his sensitive love of nature as just noted in prior quotes, and in *"Downstream, water birds / wade its weedy banks / catch minnows..."* and also *"The patter of gentle April rains / sprinkles the assurance / of silken milkweed parachutes...."*

If one knows of the reflections of Native American Spirituality one is wise beyond years. Many Native Americans believe that the Creator has planted a sacred tree under which all the Peoples may gather to be reminded of the good given to all people like compassion, patience, wisdom, courage, humility, and other gifts. In one of Richard's briefest poems *"Unity"* he likewise writes *"the only difference / I can see / between you and me / is me."* How wise can a poet be!

Enjoy Richard's insightful offerings in these poems: *The Poet, Mountain Breathing, River,* and *Brave Voice,* among others. They give us much to savor indeed.

Preface

Over the course of my writing career, I had over three hundred of poems published in anthologies, chap books, five collections of my poetry, and most especially in *Ann Arbor Review*. The editor of *Ann Arbor Review* liked my work, and I became a regular contributor. Often, if I hadn't submitted anything, he'd write to ask if I had a poem or two for an upcoming issue.

The poems in this volume were originally published in *Ann Arbor Review*. A few found their way into other publications or into one of my poetry collections. However, the majority of these made their first and only appearance in *Ann Arbor Review: International Journal of Poetry*, as it is formally called. Yet among them, I believed, was some of my best work. To rectify this, the theme I chose for this volume of collected poems was my entire catalog of poetry published in *Ann Arbor Review*.

In curating this volume, I decided not to organize poems by the dates of first publication, but to arrange them to lend a narrative flow to the book. Since the magazine was founded in Ann Arbor, Michigan, it felt natural to open the collection with a poem about students there, follow that with additional poems inspired by time spent in that region, and then move on to other subjects and areas of the world.

The poems are of two distinct styles, short, koan-like observations, or longer story-like poems that may be imaginary or a memory. Neither form is indicative of the year in which I created the poem, as I continue to write in both styles. Over the decades that these poems span, I experimented with different styles, rhythms, and voices. Years spent studying meditation and eastern philosophy frequently comes through in ontological poems.

In addition to poetry that appeared in *Ann Arbor Review*, I have included a bonus of six new poems that are slated for forthcoming issues that hadn't come out by the time this manuscript went to press.

It has been an honor to have had some of my best poems accepted by such an esteemed poetry journal.

—Richard Gartee

Arboretum Daze

The good citizens of A-squared,
lie quietly tucked in their dreams,
while we race down the snowy hills
of the arboretum
on cardboard toboggans
made from discarded boxes
scavenged from the loading dock
of an appliance store.

Drunk on Meister Brau
bought for fifty-cents a quart
and laughing our asses off
we climb back up the hill
and do it again, and again
until the dawn paints the snow
with pink and orange tinges.

As we abandon our cardboard
and drift home, our shoes crunching
the freshly fallen layer of snow
workers on the morning shift
follow a snowplow down Washtenaw Avenue.

Stripping off our icy socks and frozen pants
we bury our toes under cheap quilts
bought at St. Vincent de Paul's or Salvation Army
and soon snore away last night's folly.

Waking, having missed our morning classes,
we head to the student union.
Over hot coffee and donuts
try to remember where we put our assignments
and decide if we should go to our afternoon class
or back to bed.

January Moon

In a blue sky
on a cold January day,
the afternoon moon hangs
gauzy as a Florentine cookie,
its bottom edge ragged
as though nibbled on
by winter starved squirrels.

The trail of a jet cuts the sky,
as if propelling the jet toward
the January moon.
But its plume is not the thrust,
only vapor left behind,
momentary marks where
the plane once was.
And soon enough
they too will fade.

I remember, before solstice,
when winter lost the light
like a candle on a leaf
set afloat on icy water,
drifting until the cold
trapped it in skim ice
and a northern wind
snuffed the flame.

Gray light filled the ensuing days
until skies grew so cold
that clouds could no longer form
to hide the January moon.

Time Koan

Without the heavens
there are no stars.
Without stars,
without sun,
without moon,
what time is it?

Spring Into Summer

Despite the proclamations
on *Game of Thrones*
Winter is not coming,
it has flown
on the wings of robins
flying north
hitchhiking on the flutter
of monarch butterflies
leaving Mexico.

The patter of gentle April rains
sprinkles the assurance
of silken milkweed parachutes
presently only just sprouted
but promised to summer solstice
all the same.

And when that sunny season
delivers on spring's pact
I shall walk the lawns
of my childhood,
pluck the hoary dandelions,
and blow their seeds into the wind
to land where they will
and sleep until another spring.

On a Shady Lane

On a shady lane, a little boy
picks dandelions, and
leaves them in sweaty bouquets
at the other end of the culvert
for the neighbor girl
who is contagious
and can't come near him
or so their mothers say

His heart wants to tear from
his chest and rush toward her
but they stand
separated by thirty feet of gravel
while the blossoms wither
and their stems curl

Purty Yellow Daisies

Mother abhorred dandelions.
A verdant croquet-court lawn
was her dream,
speckles of yellow-headed weeds
her dread.

Her health wasn't good,
but on summer days when
she felt up to it,
she'd be out in the yard
with a hoe or a spade
digging up dandelions.
If the kids were around,
she'd make them help.

Kids held the opposite opinion
regarding dandelions,
considering them to be
a resource of endless pleasure.

A kid could rub a blossom
under his sister's chin,
and turn her skin yellow.

Hollow dandelion stems,
easily slipped,
one end into the other,
to make bracelets and
long green necklaces.
Stems split lengthwise,
formed tight curls.

→

Best of all, came the days
when dandelions turned
hoary-headed.
Delightful to blow on,
watching a hundred seeds
take flight
like white-winged fairies.

The hardware store sold
a special garden tool
called a dandelion puller.
It had a long handle like a hoe
with a fork-shaped end
that slipped under the base
of the plant and pulled it up
by the roots.
It's hard know what became
of that dandelion puller.
It never kept up with the
proliferation of seeds.

One year, when her cause
was clearly lost, and
her yard polka-dotted yellow,
a door-to-door salesman rang.
Thinking to ingratiate himself to
the lady of the house with a compliment,
he said, "My, your yard is just filled
with purty yellow daisies."

As much as Mother abhorred dandelions,
in that moment
she detested that salesman more.
Without a word of explanation,
she slammed the door in his face.
He left the porch and walked
across the lawn to the next house. →

Along the way, he stooped down,
picked a pretty yellow blossom,
and wondered what he'd said wrong.

Fifteen

Fifteen is delicate,
the fragrance of summer clouds
in the thunder.

Soda Fountain Days

One hand slapping time
on the green Formica countertop
to Ricky Nelson on the juke box
—Well, hello Mary Lou…
the other hand absently spinning
an empty stool, round and round.
Ricky fades, gears whir, platters change
—You can't sit down…
A poodle skirt brushes against his hand, "I can't?"

His eyes jerk up,
the brunette with a shoulder-length page boy
from geometry.
Oh, God, was he subconsciously singing aloud?
Fire races up his cheeks.
He yanks his hand off the stool
which continues to whirl.
She halts it with her bare knee.
He notices the knee,
stocking stopping just below it,
hemline hovering just above it

In one fluid movement,
she drops her books on the counter,
sweeps her forearm under her skirt, and sits.

He studiously focuses on the gray pate
of tightly permed curls reflected
in the mirrored wall behind the counter,
on the woman bent deep in the frost rimmed freezer
scooping hard packed ice cream into fluted glass dishes
and chrome milk shake cups
while cold vapor escapes around her short arms.

His blushing visage is in the reflection, too,
and next to that, a girl wearing
a pink Orlon sweater, a size too small.
Or intentionally bought like that?
Either way doesn't matter; it's the same effect.

The old lady turns from the freezer case
and asks what she wants
"Vanilla Coke."
"Large or small?"
...a quick glance his way, "Large, please."
She gives her best cheerleader smile.

The waitress doesn't care, it's been twenty years
since she'd been the girl on the stool.
Her motions are routine,
shovel ice in the Coke glass,
pump the syrup plunger with her palm,
put the glass under the chrome spigot,
pull on its black Bakelite handle.

Soda water rushes out in a noisy torrent, washing
the thick syrup off the ice cubes in brown eddies.
From under the counter materializes a bottle of vanilla,
a couple of shakes, a few drops fall,
then a quick stir with a long silver spoon.
She sets the glass on a paper lace doily
and lays a straw next to it, "15 cents."
Carbonation bubbles effervesce above the rim.

The girl fiddles with the gold clasp on her change purse.
He swivels a quarter turn in her direction and eyes the Coke
wishing for all the world he knew the magic to change it
into a malt with two straws.

Flying in Eights

When you jump out of an airplane,
falling feels almost like flying,
until the chute doesn't open.

Flap your arms and cry out, knowing
you won't end the plummet intact.

Slammed, like a hurling shot-put,
the dirt doesn't taste like it did,
that time you ate it as a kid.

The Lion Has Flown

Emma sent a text
to say her father passed
in early morning.

Knowing him, he probably
grumbled that the sun wasn't even up,
but for certain,
with his departure from the mortal coil,
the sun has set
on a wild fire.

Although some remember
him as a postal worker,
we who knew him "when,"
recall his fiery chariot
tearing across the skies
in his best imitation of Apollo.

A Leo devouring goddesses;
a minstrel plucking strings in E modal tuning;
a jester tossing off quips;
a shaman telling stories,
some true, some not.

Tonight, I look up
and see a meteor streak
across the starry sky,
or maybe it is him,
burning brightly one more time.

Last Lovers In Burgundy Province

The village,
pastel from sunlight diffused
by a sheer veil
of cloud,

trees,
black stalks, barren, tall;
gentled, lent charisma,
by the contrast with
brown-russet bricks;

naked limbs over-watch aged
buildings four stories high.

White cloud light
brilliant on the windowpanes
glints from upper-story apartments
like afternoon shimmering off
an old man's spectacles.

Hot breath in a room,
second row from the top,
frosts windows.

While city eyes turn down
into their cups
last of all, two young lovers
make-out.

The damp chill of autumn
has bitten deep the others,
it holds them apart.
Alone they scurry
over winter fit streets

or crawl,
asleep, into their minds.

At sunrise the discards
of wine lie in spills on
the cafe floor
while three stories above
a last candle burns low;
in purple village shade
nothing seems left
but shadows of morning,
and lavender streets cooled too soon.

Found Naked Lunch

Enlighten me
with your brilliant mind.

Carry on alone
singing softly.

Pretend to be a body
healthy with brains.

Health in absentia.

River

The river starts wide,
then enters a chasm that narrows it.
Channeled between rocky walls,
its intensity increases,
cutting deep,
carving a canyon to make its bed.

Sleep no more lazy river,
suffer mighty torrents
rasping sandstone and granite alike
for a millennia or two.

Crystals of mica ripped from muscovite
sparkle like drops of water spray
effervescing from rapids in sunlight.

The tumult foams like tailings
of suds from an old fashion washboard.

Reaching the canyon's end
it becomes what all tyrants fear,
aware of its confinement.

Feeling the impending open plain,
rocks crumble at the ravine's edges
as the waters rush out; the river
broadens and recomposes itself.

Downstream, water birds
wade its weedy banks
catch minnows
but never venture upstream
into the turbulent canyon roar.

Mountain Breathing

1.
    We follow a guide
    along her exact path
    step into each space
    she has just left;
    one foot to the other.

    the song of each nostril
    pulses with rarified air.
    we reach at last, a mountain-top meadow.

2.
    Feet breathe rocks
    of the path.
    we follow light
    scattered through our breasts
    from an afternoon sun;

    taste the chilled ozone
    as we near the summit.

3.
    Moist field seems a
    yellow-delicate green altar
    honoring the process of
    balance and the process of
    law governing the turn
    of an atom
    or the evening of a planet.

4.
    Inhaling great waves of light
    the Earth breathes twice
    each year.

We have walked up to see the exhalation
begin.

Hearing the transition
take place, in
no more than a breath of seasons.

5.
   Eyes close,
   waiting in stillness.

   We transcend even our own noisy
   self
   for this second,
   within
   as the current of life to death changes.

   We stay
   watching the hesitation
   of breath thought
   on a September mountain
   when the aspens are gold
   and yellow Summer tips
   the scale to Fall
   Sun hides golden rays
   behind taller trees
   Sapphire sky turns surprisingly cold

6.
   Tentative, wary, observers reluctantly rise
   to descend
   weightless from balance

   No one shall
   be on this altar mountain to see in
   the breathless death,
   of Winter.

The Deva

Fairy winds give flight
and a petite creature
with peacock-colored dragonfly wings
ascends on thermal currents
to its aerie on distant mountaintop
where morning frost sugars its nest
in air so thin the sun has no filter
and ultraviolet rays can pink bare flesh
with a moments exposure.

Below, calving ice
cracks like thunder
and avalanches white darkness
over the lower meadows
causing tiny bluebells to
wear snowflake hats and shiver.

The world turns one degree
and fingers of sunlight
extend across the valley floor.
Frozen crystals become puddles
mirroring the fuchsia sunrise
and Teton peaks.

A fawn noses aside a clump of snow
to nibble the spring grasses
flattened by the unexpected
slide of the powdery blanket.

The doe stands nearby
eying the vale
alert for shadowy movement
sniffing the cool air for predators

Above the timberline
the deva leans out
surveys the scene below
and slides from her nest
gliding on diaphanous wings
descends in lazy circles

Landing amidst a patch of baby's breath
she inclines against a willowy stem.
Startled, the doe gives a soft call
bringing the fawn to her side.

The sun blooms full
making the field luminous.
A hummingbird arrives
and the deva flits away.

Bananas for Baba

The old man in an Indian dhoti
dodders the dusty Madurai street
leaning on a walking stick
nearly as tall as he is.

As we approach
he lurches toward me
pointing to his mouth
saying "buh, buh."
I shake my head no
and keep walking.

Another day I almost trip
as he stabs his gnarled staff
into the tan sand at my feet
to hold himself erect.
Where it strikes the earth
clouds of dust spring up
and hover around my ankles.
Again, he begs, "buh, buh."

One morning, I think of him
and bring a banana from breakfast.
I walk up behind him
and say, "Baba,"
(respected elder).
He turns.
I offer the banana.
He seizes it.

Next day I take him another banana
but can't find him.
I think, Well, I've missed him.
Then, at the last minute he is
before me.
" Baba," I call to him,
hand him the banana,
and decide,
in the future I shall
always bring a banana.

A day comes that he isn't there.
Has something happened?
Did the old man collapse somewhere
never to cross my path again?
Should I give his banana
to some other worthy soul
who hungers in the morning light?

What could I do?
I save his banana.

Three days I carry that banana.
Its skin too dark
for me to take home
and put back in the fruit bowl.

I recall a Zen story
called *Eating The Blame,*
and wonder if I'm going to have to
eat the banana myself.

Then, I spy Baba
standing in the road.
His eyes lock mine.
I shout and run to him,
black banana in hand   →

It is soft and warm,
almost banana pudding inside its peel.

A large bus hurls toward us
honking furiously,
missing us by millimeters,
miring us in clouds of dust.

I lay the black wonder in his palm
and hurry off without
looking back to see
what he thought of it.

Tea in Goa

I order coffee
and the boy brings a silver pot.
"May I pour?" he says.
Something weak and pale
streams from the spout.

I add milk
& the color wanes to moonlight.
I sip.
It's tea.
He returns and I tell him,
"I ordered coffee."
"You want powder?" he replies.
"No. Thanks. I'll drink the tea."

I return to my room and change for the pool.
When I come out a cyclone of bees
swirls out from the base of a tree and upward.
I sidestep them and go looking for the lobby
but find the library instead.
I peruse their books and choose a likely candidate.
When I return the bees are gone.

At the pool
a cat the color of yellow Portuguese houses
saunters by
perambulating his domain.
He apparently is the proprietor.

The pool is languid.
I rest my head on the edge
& let my feet float weightless.
My mainspring unwinds
and time stops.   →

A man with a British accent
sits at a table in the shade.
It's just the two of us until
a pretty French mother brings her young son.
She has refined cheeks and a petite nose.
The boy is naked, but the French don't mind.
She smiles at me with azure eyes
 and even white teeth.

Lounging on a deck chair
I read,
glancing at her occasionally.
The afternoon light
reflecting off ripples
in the pool water produces
an aurora borealis effect
on the trees overhead.

Two women come, then two more.
Four men follow.
Suddenly the pool is no longer our own.
No more aurora borealis.
No more French fantasy.

A jumble of foreign syllables
spin around me
but I can't sort out the country of origin.
One of the women says "Hello,"
but that is the extent of her English.
She looks Israeli.

One of the men has a soccer ball.
The eight newcomers form a circle in the water
men on one half, women on the other.

→

Tossing the ball,
chasing each other,
finding excuses to dunk the guys,
or nudge the girls,
like an adult version of spin-the-bottle.

Soon the separation between opposite sexes
dissolves like suntan lotion in chlorine water.
In no time they are paired off
and repair from the pool, like
they'd known each other a lifetime.
Ahh the magic of Goa.

The waiter brings drinks to the men
and a silver pot with cup and saucer to the Israeli
woman.
It makes me think of coffee,
yet I feel certain it is tea,
though we lack the lingua franca to discuss it,
her and I.
A crow lands on her table and
begins sipping her milk.
I point this out to her,
but she doesn't understand me.
Finally her girlfriend notices
and they laugh.

The tabby returns
sips water from the pool edge
eyeing the strangers.
He doesn't mind.
He's seen all this before
and neither approves nor disapproves,
but simply wanders on his intended way.

→

Strolling to my room,
the gods have strewn
flowers at my feet.
Delicate white blossoms
with pale yellow centers
have fallen over the pathway.
Their mild, milky color
reminds me of morning tea in Goa.

Shakespeare's Garden

Outside the bard's window
a scarlet blossom droops,
sagged and browning,
battered by too many
thoughts about it.
On a thorny stem, lame from
the weight of too many metaphors,
the bent flower head whimpers,
> Oh, poet, choose some other
> bloom in this garden
> to bruise with your similes.
But the bard cannot hear
or does not choose to listen.

First Revelation

While one with mother,
essentials flowed freely
and abundantly.
Never gave it a thought.

Suddenly, life's first revelation:
what we want is outside of us
and requires effort to get it.
What a slap on the ass, that was!

Breathe in
breath out
don't stop
not even to sleep.

Take a nap,
wake up, cry for mother,
latch on, suckle, swallow, burp,
then fall back asleep.

And the wanting?
There seems no end to it.
Buddha warned that'd be
the problem.

Stay Seated

The sun does not leave
its seat in heaven
yet daylight comes in morning
and departs at night

The river does not flow
inland from the ocean
but empties into the sea

The world moves
the mind creates thoughts
consciousness does not
have to go to them
to notice them float by
like bubbles on a passing stream

Four Lines for Ken

ego–death
like water is
strange &
guiltless.

Stillpoint

He sits still,
perfectly at rest,
while everything else
is in motion

Bosons and leptons
and quarks move,
but He does not
move in mysterious ways,
or in any way

Eternally conscious stillness
watching the big bang unfold.

Old Order

Reading aloud about convent life
she left decades earlier,
a former nun stands at the podium.

Gray hair cascades over her shoulders
like an old style habit.
Her clothing, black and white,
serves as a subconscious remainder
of clothes she'd worn fifteen years or longer.

She asks our permission to read more.
Given the nod, she continues
with descriptive passages about
women's voices ringing in the sacred space
of a marble choir loft,
and concludes with: "women are givers of life,
arms encircling a well reflecting stars and moon,
 symbols of the universe."

Brave Voice

The poet's dark chocolate eyes
stare out her apartment window,
through a hard tropical rain, watching
the canal behind her building overflow.
The canal where sometimes alligators lie
when they find their way from the Everglades
into someone's backyard;
where they wait for a small tasty dog
or a girl poet on her way to a poetry slam.
Not her of course—she's a woman, not a girl.
She ain't afraid of no gator
(even if channel 7 keeps running those stories)
And she's not going to stand here,
peering through rain streaked glass,
imagining one out there.

In a room of friends and strangers,
she prepares to throw forth words
peeled from her naked heart
one night in the dark.
Pausing to worry, what's this weather done to her hair?
She slips her tongue
between plush lips,
clears her throat,
and begins to read a poem
she wrote when she was fifteen,
before she ever met a gator.

Fame

To be famous,
a "Somebody" in the public's mind
is coin easily squandered,
a fiction time forgets.

Infamy, however, is
like that piece of toilet paper
stuck on the sole of your shoe,
trailing behind as you exit
a public restroom.

Semi-Native

So many flee the northern realms,
forwarding address: Miami Beach
where it's always ninety degrees,
and sun shines even while it's raining.

Here, beach girls smell of coconut oil
as they lie on sandy blankets
with the straps of their bikinis
unfastened.

On South Beach, Ferraris and Lamborghinis
vie for parking outside swanky clubs;
inside, anorexic women in skin-tight dresses
and stiletto heels twerk to Cuban rhythms.

Meanwhile, in Key West,
the tourists drink margaritas,
sing Karaoke about a broken flip-flop,
and pay homage to Papa at Sloppy Joe's.

Snowbirds swear they miss the four seasons
with the scent of spring lilacs
and children licking
mulberry purpled fingers.

Apparently, they've forgotten
shoveling out the driveway,
stepping into ankle deep slush,
or March coming in like a lion.

Those who forgo seasonal migrations,
in favor of permanent residence,
invest in license plates
that read: Semi-Native.

Lost and Found Shoes

The closest parking space is a couple of blocks away.
There never is any parking downtown.
I get out and opened the car door for her.

She does a quarter turn in her seat
and slides her slim ankles out the door.
Black straps no wider than fettuccine
hold her latest fashion acquisition on narrow feet.

My date has a thing for shoes;
a plethora of which clog her closets.
Whenever we go out, she obsessively notices
what shoes other women are wearing.

We are walking toward the theater district
when we come upon
a woman's high-heel shoe on the sidewalk.
Its companion lies in the grass a few feet away.

She stops. I sense her reluctance to pass the orphaned
   footwear.
She picks up the shoe from the concrete and looks it
   over.
It's very dressy.

A subtle sadness comes over her. To her mind,
Shakespeare couldn't have devised a more lamentable
   tragedy
than this beautiful pair of shoes should be lost or
   abandoned.

She speculates that the woman may have been taken—
   plucked right out of her shoes.
That seems unlikely to me, and I say so.

Abducted by whom—aliens in flying saucers?
She pushes me away, annoyed.

I pick up the second shoe and postulate a more
   reasonable scenario:
the woman had worn walking shoes
and carried her high heels
in her bag like New Yorkers do.
Perhaps they'd fallen out.

My date isn't convinced. She wants us to take the shoes to...
I don't know where,
some lost and found for sidewalks?
some random nightclub in the city?

I pry the first shoe from her hand and place it
and its mate on the walk,
reasoning that if the person who lost them comes back,
we should leave them where they can be easily found.

Some say a man is a creature of reason, and woman an
   emotional soul,
never has that been more evident than when
I make her leave a pair of lost shoes behind.

Fingering The Jam

Anna Marie and Nancy fingering the jam
dancing over the frets between G and D.

Brushing a curl from her eye Anna Marie sings, while
Nancy, bending the strings, sets the stage afire
triple timing every measure
fingers flying so fast notes are dropping on the floor.
The bass player's driving.
The drummer's breaking sticks.

Swiveling her volume knob down,
Nancy lets the guitar fall off
so we can hear Anna Marie,
who grabs the microphone
flicks her tongue across her lips,
opens her mouth, and lets rip.
The crowd jumps to its feet.
She grins at Nancy, and Nancy grins back.
Two goddesses of rock & roll,
brown-eyed as Van Morrison's girl
in the stadium lights
with their amplifiers jacked.

Summer Breeze

She blew through
like a Caribbean trade wind
carrying the scent of jasmine.
Wearing a gossamer dress
that swirled above her knees
revealing suntanned thighs
the color of coffee with cream,
she stole the eyes
of every man
and the ire of their ladies.

She said her name was Summer Breeze,
and whilst men stared and women glared,
neither could hear the music that moved
her hips in sultry whirls
that stirred the air into a summer breeze.

Laurel Canyon Houri

With a pink lacquered fingernail
she snags a gossamer scarf
wraps it thrice around her waist
and pulls it lower to make sure she's covered.
Bare breasted she walks into the kitchen
touches a button on the electric kettle,
in ninety seconds water boils.
She pours it into her French press,
carries it out onto the open balcony,
and sets it on the small, round, glass table.
She goes to the railing and gazes over Laurel Canyon.
A shirtless man strumming his guitar on the deck
of a house in the canyon below, looks up and waves.
She waves back, turns, and pushes the plunger
of the coffee press.
Filling her cup, she holds it toward him
with gesture of invitation.
He nods and sets his guitar in its case.

Fifteen minutes later he is at her door,
shiny with sweat from the steep climb.
She puts on an iridescent bandeau
fit for a Tahitian dancer or Persian houri,
opens the door and bids him, enter.
She saunters back onto the patio,
hips undulating in graceful sway.
His eyes follow, then his feet.

She pours him a coffee and refills her own.
He lifts it to his lips, inhales its fragrant aroma,
and takes a sip. She does the same.

A lazy cloud drifting overhead
creates a slowly moving patch of shadow
which meanders over the canyon foliage
and winding roads below.
Life is good, full of potential.
A soft breeze flutters strands of her hair across her face.
She brushes them back with her hand
in an subconscious motion.
They discuss laws of attraction and detachment,
heady stuff for breakfast.
He leans over to kiss her. She leans away.
He says, "Don't lead me if you don't want to go."
She lifts one eyebrow, and smiles,
confident as any master of Kublai's pleasure dome,
      "Were you writing a song about me?"
He blushes and looks flustered.
Her eyes cut a glance downhill,
and with a wave of her lacquered nails,
he is dispatched home to finish her paean.

Last Dance of the Year

The band,
play list exhausted,
are starting to repeat themselves,
but they can't quit now,
it's only minutes 'til midnight.
So they sing a song of Mary Jane;
not exactly Auld Lang Syne,
but they never knew what those lyrics
meant anyway.

On this night the girls,
in their tightest dresses,
made their boyfriends make an effort;
"Put on a nice shirt, dear."

One more song as everyone holds on.
Then seconds to count
10, 9, 8...
and the old one's gone.

Lovers, strangers,
and estranged lovers
kiss.

The planet commences another
waltz around the sun.

To Wish Again Upon A Star

We arrive at our first kiss
with scars that weigh against
our longings.

Lovers past, some forgotten,
raised welts on our hearts
leaving invisible marks.

Memories of past failures
pale in the bright spark
that leaps the gap
as lips approach,
before they touch.

Electric anticipation
cauterizes bygone wounds.
Hope becomes all.

Reason, logic, are swept absent
as pulse hastens
and blood surges.

New love hovers
a breath away,
the air between us
tingling.

A shooting star
suspended in space
waits to fall.

He and She

She was like ice at the point of melting,
ephemeral, impossible to pick up.

He was like negative space in art,
unseen, though it surrounded her
and defined her edges.

Rubin's illusion
Two faces or a single vase,
that described their relationship,
in black and white.

They met on a cold spring day
that should have been hot.
Flowers that had opened early
in the warm Southern light
shivered and shriveled
at the unseasonable change.

She, who could bring
an unconscious room
to life by entering it,
was like troubled waters.

He, with no desire to be newly fashioned,
found himself to be fresh dirt in the hands
of an eager landscaper.

Life together promised to be a lush valley
between high mountains,
but every raindrop and snowflake
sooner or later slides downward;
and rough waters are not quieted
by flash floods and avalanches.

Blinds and Shutters

At school, the wife had learned
the ancient Roman saying,
"The eyes are windows to the soul."
Taking it for truth
she'd since made of her eyelids
Venetian blinds
canting them like angled slats
to block would be voyeurs
from espying her immortal Self.

By the time she married
she wore mascara layered so thick that
peering out through half-closed eyes
was like looking
through prison bars
of her own making.

The husband waited
while she put on her makeup
for their anniversary dinner.
Her mascara brush reminded him
of a rat tail dragged through a tar pit
as she loaded it with black goo
and trawled through her lashes.

She caught the judgment in his eye,
leaned her head against his,
and said into his ear,
"Will yourself not to speak."

→

A tear slithered
from the edge of her
Venetian blinds
and slid like a spider
down a cord
but her face was too close to his
for him to see the teardrop
that felt like dew,
dampening his cheek.

Through her prison bar perception
she noticed hair growing in his ears;
not soft, pale, peach fuzz,
but wild, unruly, cactus spikes
that sprang in every direction
and required no mascara
to make them thick and black.

She straightened the slats
of her Venetian eyes
to confirm her perception
wasn't a deception
of her own makeup.

No, there were definitely tufts
jutting from his ear canals,
thickets that begged to be cut,
by her, if he would let her.
She wondered
why men of a certain age
suddenly grew hirsute fields
in ears otherwise pink as conch shells.
Perhaps the shag in his ears
acted as aural shutters
sheltering him against criticisms
he'd tired of hearing.

→

His finger brushed the ear
where her whisper had tickled.
She pulled her face even with his eyes
and let him have a look through her open blinds;
the first time in forty years.

He, finally permitted to see into her eyes,
didn't see her soul
or her notions about ear stubble,
only his own worrisome thoughts
about being late to the restaurant.

She blotted her lipstick and nodded.
He draped her shawl over her shoulders
and they walked outside.
He started to lock the door,
but she stayed his hand,
and stepped back inside,
to close the blinds.

Madwife

I put my key into the lock
and turned the door knob
ever so gently
it swung open soundlessly,
the hinges did not squeak.
I took off my shoes and
stepped into the foyer
thorns stuck in my feet
anniversary flowers strewn
everywhere on the floor.

The roses were yellow
but her face was red
the vase laid in shatters
crystal shards splayed
down the hall
there I stood
with a thorn in my foot
and a bottle of wine
in my hand
daggers flying from
her eyes.

Three dead soldiers
in the trash
and a glass half empty
in her hand.

I've no idea what
I've done, but
I must have done
it again.

If I had the brains
of an armadillo
I'd turn right around.
Instead I step into the abuse
because you know fools
come in twos.
Celebration must have
started early and without me
but something turned sour
in her mind between
the second and third bottle
while I was still at work
now she's pissed
in all meanings of the word.
A colander of cold spaghetti
looks like brains in the sink
Sauce in a blue enameled pot
congealed.
A pan of garlic rolls
sits next to it, half baked
an accusation waiting
to happen.

Enuf

When love is not enuf
tho each had vowed it would be
traitors of the heart
trickster of slippery ghosts
of past promises that can't
be seen in foresight but
only hover in peripheral vision.

Things start reasonable,
the head reaching beyond itself
feels good.
Love wants to expand
toward others
but trying too hard to be
 in two places at once
ends up not being in either place.

After forty years, one of them asks,
Why does the hamster
stay on the wheel?
The other answers,
Because from inside the cage
it feels like somewhere to go.

The Mind

The mind
is a small
place to live.

Grasses and Houses

The silent drone
          of humming hands
      that fills the endless sea
                of tears
     and sweat
covers the ears
           in deadly glaze
  of golden mists
    and raindrops
gone

the roaring thunder
            of the crushing waves
            as they smash against
            little grains of sand
            laying like a golden carpet
            beneath the foam
pounds against the ear drum

The heavy feet
        no one hears
trip clumsily
        over the neatly weaved branches
        that formed the small grass house
we slept in last summer

The umbrae shades
        pulled tightly down
        over the window of sunshine
     and the stars
          like tiny holes
             in the black paper
flickered
    in unison

                with the lap,
                            of the water
and I fell into your lap,
flickering in unison
                        on the golden carpet

But now the white dry sand
                            scorched and yellow
                        by the fire of the day

lies
        still warm
            beneath my bare toes
            and the grass house
            is a mangled bunch of weeds
under the black summer sky.

Ever New Morning

Wake up in the fuchsia light
of morning without anything
from the previous day
hanging over.

Wake up without
a preconceived way
today should unfold.

Wake up with appreciation
of the unfolding experiences
that appear as your eyes open.

Wake up and live fully
what the day will be
then sleep without anticipation
the next new morning.

Clouds

Imagine being the sun,
and light rays,
consciousness
streaming forth.

On that which the sunbeams come to rest,
become the objects of which we are aware.

Between sun and object,
    space.
A gap midst which
clouds can arise,
as sunlight evaporates sea
and atmosphere cools
molecules of water to coalesce
around particles of dust.

Its umbra reduces light
that reaches objects below.
And in the clouds' shapes,
imaginary figures distract
our awareness.

The clouds may darken,
hiding the sun
until it rains.

The clouds dissipate,
the storm is done.
With clouds gone,
sun shines without obstruction.

Unity

the only difference
    I can see
between you and me
is me.

Cornfield Christmas

The bearded shepherd
        drifts past
the hustling shoppers
        rushing to buy

As the strings of tinsel
            drip from the wires
            and lamp posts
he wanders from the concrete
        into the meadow
            now covered
            with cold and snow

he looks
        at the desolate cornfield and by the flicker
        of a dimming star
        sees the Christmas.

Sense and Probability

(after Plato)

The world as created,
is apprehended by our senses.
Fashioned after the eternal pattern;
an eternal pattern can be
spoken of with certainty.
The created copy can only be described
in the language of probability.

Un-Platonic Solids

The roof changed pitch sixteen times,
a wild experiment,
a builder stretching himself,
extending his skills,
but knowing nothing about Feng Shui.

Shape twisted energy at such odd angles
that no one could live
in that space for long.
And no one did.

Constructed of cedar beams
that wouldn't rot,
the building hung around
and hung around.

Forty years later,
it sagged at angles
even stranger than its architect imagined.
Finally, men who built it
had to pull it down.

The oddity dismantled
the lot scraped clean,
traces of it erased.

But when the forest returns,
what if mans' triangles
left space at the site bent?

New trees might grow at crazy angles,
reminding us
where the oddity once stood.

Nothing Out of Something

There's too much stuff in my office,
especially on my desk.
A jar of pens collected at conferences
years ago
three-quarters of which probably
dried up, are useless.
But how to tell? Try each one?
That could take all day.

I start with the burgundy plastic
in/out basket of papers
which continue to come in
and fail to go out
becoming an archeological site,
layered geological strata
like rock formations in Utah.
"Tell me when you sent that
and I'll know how deep
in the pile to look."

I move on to the file cabinet
its overstuffed drawers
protruding papers
that keep them from closing fully.
Edging the bottom drawer open
wide enough for my hand to fit
I mash the mess down and
slam the drawer shut before the files
leap out in rebellion.

I refill my coffee cup,
return to my office,
and ponder my situation.

Plainly, I have too many papers.
The needed solution:
How to make nothing
out of too much something?
Fahrenheit 451 comes to mind.
But then my eye fall on a page
containing a few lines of verse
I think, This bit of nothing could become something.
So, I add it to a future pile and postpone cleaning
my office for another day.

Inspiration

You are just the person present
at the moment there is inspiration.

Loitering outside the opening
Blake called the door of perception.

Then, a smoking goddess
opens the stage door a crack,
tosses out a lit cigarette butt,
and in seconds
the back alley of your mind
becomes a conflagration,
a creative flash fire.

Bat Kol, the feminine voice of God
arises,
and if you're in her service,
you write down what she says,
and then she goes away.

Refine yourself, and the Bat Kol
recognizes that you are open.
She arrives. You speak.
She departs.

The Poet

Intensifying, illuminating
everyday events
the poet studies what others
have passed by
and brings them back
to that
which they have lost.

About the Author

Richard Gartee has had over three hundred of poems published in anthologies, chapbooks, and six volumes of collected poems. He is also an award-winning novelist who authored seven novels, seven college textbooks, a biography, and a book on the history of the Hippodrome Theatre.

    A complete list of his available titles, upcoming events, and forthcoming books is available at www.gartee.com where you can find links to purchase his books, and sign up to receive updates on his newest publications as they become available.

Visit gartee.com

Additional Poetry by Richard Gartee

Mountain Breathing

Collected Poems Volume 2

in paperback and e-book

ISBN: 978-0-9895104-4-8

Mountain Breathing is a collection of 66 poems spanning four decades that form a study in the evolution of a poet philosopher with feet made of sand, whose soul may sing OM, but whose eyes notice blond hairs on the back of tan thighs at the beach. Along the way are observations of how we think, feel, and interact with the people who appear in our lives, and with the universe unseen.

Watching Waves

Collected Poems Volume 3

in paperback and e-book

ISBN: 978-0-9895104-5-5

Watching Waves is a collection of poems comprised almost entirely of deeply personal interior musings about the nature of reality. Over eighty percent of this collection has never appeared in print before. Themes of a universal God and our search for God are prevalent throughout. Diverse influences of Indian Gurus, Tibetan Lamas, Lao Tzu, Zen, Sufi and Christian mystics inform the book's cosmology

Canyon Falls

Collected Poems Volume 4

in paperback and e-book

ISBN: 978-0-9895104-7-9

Canyon Falls is a collection of poems about love and relationships using the imagery of two distinct metaphors. It is about the moment we know we are about to fall in love, when the breath stops, but the heart races. The future appears beautiful, like the view from a canyon's rim. Sometimes we peek over the precipice and step back. Sometimes we jump in feet first anyway seeking that powerful energy of love flowing like a waterfall at the canyon's heart.

Humorous Fiction by Richard Gartee

Ragtime Dudes at the World's Fair

in paperback and e-book

ISBN 978-0-9895104-0-0

It's 1904. St. Louis, birthplace of the hottest new music craze, Ragtime, is hosting a World's Fair that everyone wants to see. Three fun-loving New York dandies being chased by two Irish boxers, meet three free-thinking sisters on the train and repeatedly at the Fair's dazzling palaces. Meanwhile, the pursuing pugilists close in.

Ragtime Dudes in a Thin Place

in paperback and e-book

ISBN 978-0-9906768-6-7

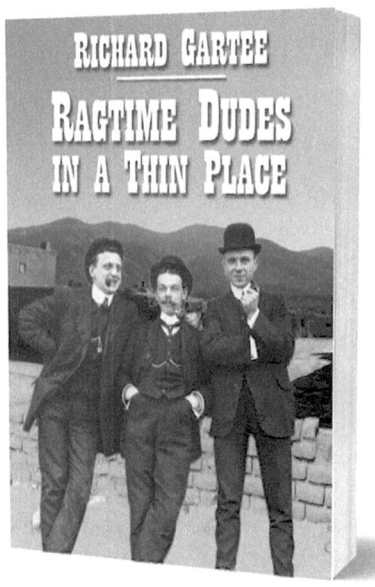

Ragtime is new, Victorians are out, and free love is on the rise when three New York dandies open an emporium in 1904 Taos, NM, where they meet more freethinking women.

Ragtime Dudes Meet a Paris Flapper

in paperback and e-book

ISBN 978-0-9906768-8-1

Ragtime is old hat, and the Roaring Twenties are underway. A Paris flapper reunites with three ragtime dudes and helps a shell-shocked soldier when the impending death of her mentor brings her back to the small town she left years ago.

Novella by Richard Gartee

Atlantis Obsession

in paperback and e-book

ISBN 978-1-7363957-4-5

Instead of writing his dissertation, PhD student Dylan Clarke becomes obsessed with Atlantis and chases his ex-girlfriend to North Africa while searching for the Eye of the Sahara.

Fantasy Fiction by Richard Gartee

Atlantis Dying

in paperback and e-book

ISBN 978-1-7363957-1-4

Climate Change threatens Atlantis. Monsoons no longer bring rain and the desert encroaches. The king and his First Consul struggle to evacuate Atlantis, thwarted by greedy barons trying to squeeze out the last smidge of profit before letting people leave..

Metaphysical Fiction by Richard Gartee

LANCELOT'S GRAIL

in paperback and e-book

ISBN 978-0-9895104-1-7

New age teachings on self-awareness and enlightenment are explored in an Arthurian-age story of two siblings' journey to enlightenment after they discover Sir Lancelot living as a hermit and uncover his knowledge of the Holy Grail.

LANCELOT'S DISCIPLE

in paperback and e-book

ISBN 978-0-9906768-1-2

After seeking self-awareness and enlightenment on the ancient Silk Road, Lancelot's disciple must sort out his confusion, attain the Holy Grail, and reconnect with his saintly sister waiting in Britain.

Nonfiction by Richard Gartee

Skating on Skim Ice

in paperback and e-book

ISBN 978-0-9906768-2-9

Like a time traveler journeying ninety-three years from the past, Dick Gartee's life from the Roaring Twenties through the age of smart phones puts America's significant transformative decades in context.

The Hippodrome Theatre First 50 Years

Hardbound in case laminate cover

ISBN 978-1-7363957-3-8

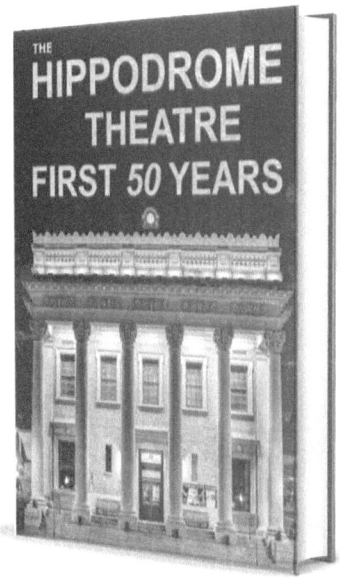

How a daring band of thespians founded a theatre that saved a dying downtown business district, became a city's cultural icon, and centerpiece of its artistic community.

www.ingramcontent.com/pod-product-compliance
Lightning Source LLC
Chambersburg PA
CBHW021120080526
44587CB00010B/579